Small Beginnings

Book of Prayers

Kathy Hendley, PhD
Jill Chapman
Jeanie Connell
Jean McMullin
Kristina Wise

Savannah House

Published by Savannah House © 2025 Kathy Hendley, PhD

Small Beginnings Book of Prayers
Kathy Hendley PhD
Jill Chapman
Jeanie Connell
Jean McMullin
Kristina Wise

Visit Savannah House publishing at www.kathyhendleyphd.org
Visit Dr. Kathy Hendley at www.kathyhendley.com

Copyright © 2025 by Kathy Hendley, LLC. All rights reserved.
Cover created by Kathy Hendley through Canva copyright © 2025. All rights reserved.

All Scripture quotations unless otherwise noted are taken from the Holy Bible New International Version,® NIV® copyright © 2011 by Biblica, Inc.®. All rights reserved worldwide wwww.Zondervan.com
Printed in the United States of America

ISBN 979-8-9921631-2-4

Dedication

To the women of Write At Home and Write on Purpose who labored over their writing and grew together in prayer

This book is dedicated to the Prayer Warriors. To all of the people who refuse to take life as it is. To the followers of Jesus who believe what He said when he told us that we can ask anything in His name and He would do it. This is your book. To those of you who get up early to get on your knees. To those of you who wake up in the middle of the night to call on the name of the Lord. To the beginning believer who wants to know how to pray, this book is for you.

A LETTER FROM THE EDITOR

Hello friend,

A few years ago, tragedy struck my family, and I found myself in a lot of pain. Along with emotional trauma, I experienced great physical pain. Doctors didn't have a lot of answers for me. My pastor, on the other hand, invited our church to a morning prayer meeting.

I resisted for months, but once I joined, everything changed.

I drank in the prayers like hot tea with honey. The words soothed my aching heart and spread into my bones and muscles. Slowly, I regained my strength. As I write this, three years later, I sit without pain - and no medications!

I met the other authors on my prayer journey. They joined me for virtual meetings, and we prayed together. The idea for this book came from those meetings. Every word you read has been carefully selected in prayer. My mom joined in on the fun of writing prayers. She has been my inspiration in the faith, and I'm happy to share her with you.

Our prayer for you is that God will change your life. We're expecting radical changes. We're asking God to transform the way you see the world. We expect miracles.

Sincerely,

Kathy Hendley

Editor

HOW TO USE

The authors came together to provide prayers and encouragement. As the editor, I had the privilege of reading each one and organizing them into topics.

Use this book as a manual and read the prayers by topic. Topics include:

How do I pray?

Praying through Psalms

Prayers from the Sermon on the Mount

Prayers for Waiting on God

Works from each author are jumbled in the mix of topics. You can identify the author of the prayer by their initials placed in the lower right corner on the title page of the prayer. Use this key to identify authors:

Kathy Hendley	KH
Jean McMullin	JM
Jill Chapman	JC
Jeanie Connell	JMC
Kristina Wise	KW

The prayers also include suggested reading or questions for reflection. If you keep a. journal, you can add this to your daily quiet time.

CONTENTS

3	A letter from the editor
4	How to use this book
9	How Do I Pray?
36	Praying Through Psalms
61	Prayers from the Sermon on the Mount
75	Prayers for Waiting on God
85	About the Authors
90	Prayers and Praises

Index of Prayers

Blessed are the Poor in Spirit	KH	62
Cease Striving	KH	28
Confessing My Sins and Seeking God's Face	KH	67
Courage to Trust	JM	80
Encouragement	JM	72
Forgive Me for the Things I Said	KH	66
Forgive Me of My Debt	KH	64
Forgiveness	KH	24
Forgiving Someone Else	KH	68
God As My Refuge and Strength	KH	44
God is Good	KH	76
Happiness	KH	37
Healing My Fears	JM	77
Healing Prayers	KH	26
Holy Armor	JMC	78
Holy Spirit	JM	81
I Repent of my Efforts to Control My Life	KH	63
Life Seems Meaningless	KH	42
Longing for the Lord	KH	43
My Enemies Pursue Me	KH	47
Peace	JM	38
Pray the Scripture	JM	13
PRAY with Jesus	KW	16
Psalms	KH	34
Remembering the Benefits of the Lord	KH	56
Repentance	KH	20
Rescue	KH	54
Roots	JMC	32
Strength From the Lord	JM	39
Thanksgiving	KH	18
The Light	JM	73
The Lord's Prayer	JC	10
Timing	JM	83

Index of Prayers

Unity in My Marriage	KH	69
Unity Through Humility	KH	70
When Evil Wins	KH	48
When I Feel Afraid	KH	40
When I Will Not Be Comforted	KH	50
Wisdom	JM	82
You Know Me	KH	58

Artwork

Isaiah 49:16	KH	65
Luke 12:27	JC	45
Micah 7:9	JC	23
Psalm 62:9	JM	15
Psalm 118:24	JC	31

How do I pray?

"Now, it came to pass, as He was praying in a certain place, when He ceased, that one of His disciples said to Him, Lord, teach us to pray..."

Luke 11:1

The Lord's Prayer

For much of my young adult life, fear controlled me with too many different types of fear to list. Fear controlled almost every aspect of my life, including my relationships, where I went, how I dressed, and what I ate. Even after I was saved and served God for years, there were times when fear controlled my actions and beliefs.

It was only when I began to see God for who He is in the scope of creation that I found deliverance. He revealed himself to me in such a way that I could no longer see myself as the center, but put him in his rightful place in my life. He delivered me from fear. Not to say that I never have any fear, but when I do, I can stand on God's promises to me.

The Lord's Prayer is one of the most beautiful examples of prayer. Of course, Jesus gave the example, so it's going to be a perfect pattern to follow. It touches on every aspect of our lives. We can trust God in all things because of who He is.

The disciples had observed Jesus and heard his teachings, which were revolutionary compared to what they'd known before they met him. They were accustomed to praying in the synagogues and listening to the prayers of rabbis. When one of the disciples asked Jesus to tell them how to pray, he was asking a deeper question. He knew how to say the words to prayers. He longed for a deeper walk with God and wanted a prayer that would meet that need.

The Lord's Prayer was Jesus' answer. He provided them with a pattern to follow in approaching God. One that we can follow, too, as we seek a closer walk.

"Our Father in heaven; hallowed be Your name."
Matthew 6:9 (NIV)

Acknowledging God as our Father is the beginning. God, our Father, the keeper of our soul. The one who loves us. Hallowed or Holy is his name. For He represents all things good, pure, and holy.

"…your kingdom come, your will be done; on earth as it is in heaven." Matthew 6:10 (NIV)

We must confess that God is in control. His kingdom is what's important. His will needs to be done, not ours.

"Give us today our daily bread." Matthew 6:11 (NIV)

The Bible tells us that all good things come from God. Asking Him to give us our daily needs is acknowledging that He is the one who meets them.

"And forgive us our debts, as we forgive our debtors."
Matthew 6:12 (NIV)

Forgiveness is a basic tenent of the Christian faith. We need forgiveness, but we also must forgive others. We should make it a daily habit to forgive others and to ask for forgiveness. This brings peace to our souls.

> **"And lead us not into temptation, but deliver us from the evil one." Matthew 6:13 (NIV)**

The world is full of temptations that would lead us away from God. Even wholesome activities can sometimes distract us from our goals as Christians. When we ask God to lead us away from temptation, it doesn't hinder our lives; it keeps us close to Him.

> **"For Thine is the kingdom, and the power, and the glory forever. Amen." Matthew 6:13b (KJV)**

The last line reminds us again who is in charge. God's omnipotence dwarfs us. His kingdom, His power, and His glory are forever. We accept and revere his superiority. He is God.

The next time you begin to pray, think of this example of prayer that Jesus gave us. Our prayers don't have to be long and eloquent. They can be short and to the point. Our goal is to pray from our heart and acknowledge God. No matter what your needs might be, mine was deliverance from paralyzing fear. He hears and answers because of his tremendous love and mercy toward us!

Suggested Reading
Matthew 6:5-15
Luke 11:1-13
John 14:5-21
1 John 5:13-16

Pray the Scripture

In 1971, I was a newlywed in a new church. I wanted to fit in with the other women. More than that, I wanted to pray. I wanted to know how to be more effective in prayer.

The Lord answered my prayer in a dream. In the dream, I was holding a Bible and reading the scripture out loud. The Lord said to pray the scripture. Say it out loud. Write it down.

Today, Lord,

Just as I need natural disciplines such as discipline to work and disciplines concerning appetites, finances, and so on, I need spiritual disciplines such as prayer, Bible study, and confessing God's Word **out loud**. This is sometimes hard for me, but I can see good results.

"I will pray to Him , and He will hear me, and I will fulfill my vows"
(Job 22:27)

Reflections

What do you need to confess to the Lord today?

What scripture comes to your mind as you sit in God's Presence?

JM

Trust God at all times, my people! Pour out your hearts to God our refuge! Psalm 62:9 NABR

Jean McMullin

PRAY with Jesus

P **Posture and Position**. If God is spirit, therefore, before you pray, you need to make sure that your spirit is in alignment with the Holy Spirit. "But when you pray, go into your room" (Matthew 6:5). Position your room, or heart, to allow God to sit with you and rule over your situation.

R **Readiness**. Paul tells us in Ephesians 6:10-11 to pray at all times. In good times or difficult situations, pray at all times. Times means any time, day or night. He continues to tell us to pray in the Spirit. The Holy Spirit intercedes (prays for us) when we don't know how to pray (Romans 8:26). Be ready to pray for any situation.

A **Availability.** Jesus was always available to pray to His Father. At any given moment and time, throughout the Gospels, we see Jesus going away to pray (Luke 9:18; Mark 8:27; Matthew 6:9-13). Being available to pray can be scary at times, but it teaches us to be like the Savior. Keep a scripture on hand and a willing spirit.

Y **Yes.** All God wants out of us is a yes in our spirit. God wants us to be willing to do whatever He asks.

Prayer

God, I thank you for all that you're doing in my life. Help me, Lord to have a position and posture to pray to you everyday. I recognize that I need you and desire to pray to your every day and over every situation.

Lord, help me to lean into You and pray more. Help me to have a heart for others and to have a heart to pray for them. I realize that it's not about me. I want to see others as You see them. I repent of my sins and ask God to open my heart to receive Your Presence. Holy Spirit, I want to have a readiness to pray wherever I am and no matter what time.

God, make me available for Your glory. Move my schedule around so I can be used by You. Move me out of the way so you can reign in my life. Make me a powerful prayer warrior for You, Jesus.

Lord, put a **Yes** in my spirit. I want to be obedient to Your commands. Help me to give, pray, and do the things You call me to do. If all You want is a **Yes**, then a **Yes** is what You will get out of me.

Suggested Readings

    Luke 11:1-11
    John 15
    Psalm 51

Thanksgiving

In my circle of friends, I refer to large meals or gatherings with people as Thanksgiving. It's a term I use to describe that joyful feeling when I see people that I love all together in one space. It's a word that describes an abundance of good food and great conversation. It's a table of delicacies, and the unusual delight that catches my attention.

These unusual delights come from God. When I give thanks, I give Him credit. Only God can bring this group of people together. God wrote that recipe, because it is divine! James tells us that every good and perfect gift comes from God (1:17). Too often, though, I take credit for it. I beam with pride when the cake turns out just right. Knowing full well that I had wrecked that recipe a dozen times in the past.

Talented writers craft prayers of thanksgiving that sound like poetry. The words rhyme and flow from our lips with an attractive cadence. Giving thanks doesn't have to be perfect and fancy. Our words of gratitude, no matter how simple, enter our Heavenly Father's ears like incense (Revelation 8:3). The prayers in this book serve as an example or starting point for your own prayers. I encourage you to add the name to the prayer. Include your own examples and make it your thanksgiving.

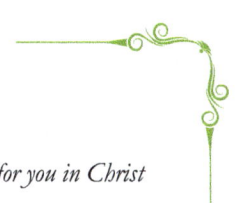

"Give thanks in everything; for this is God's will for you in Christ Jesus" *(1 Thessalonians 5:16.)*

Reflections

What are you thankful for today?

List some difficult times from the past that you have overcome.

Give thanks to the Lord for helping you through.

Repentance

"We must pay the most careful attention, therefore, to what we have heard, so that we do not drift away. For since the message spoken through angels was binding, and every violation and disobedience received its just punishment, how shall we escape if we ignore so great a salvation?"
Hebrews 2:1-3

Repentance is a church word that means to turn away from sin. It comes from the word penitent, which describes humble or painful sorrow for causing an offense. We have all been born into a sinful world and walk around with sin inside us (Romans 3:23). Sin is offensive to God. When we come to Christ, we recognize our sin and ask his forgiveness. We feel the sorrow for our sin because the Spirit of God brings it to our attention. In prayers for repentance, we confess that sorrow back to God.

The prefix "re" at the front of the word "repentance" refers to a turning away from the offense. Not only are we sorry for our sin, but we have decided to turn away from it. We don't want to continue in a life of sin. Prayers of repentance include asking God for help. In our present state, we can't stay away from sin. We require the help of the Holy Spirit to make it happen.

KH

We also pray for the Holy Spirit to reveal our sin. The journey of the Christian life is a slow process. Our transformation into the image of Christ takes time (Romans 8:29). Our prayers of repentance invite the Holy Spirit to show us the next step in the process. He will reveal places of growth and how to get there.

"For this God foreknew he also predestined to be conformed to the image of his Son, that he might be the firstborn among many brothers and sisters. And those he predestined, he also called; those he called, he also justified; those he justified, he also glorified." Romans 8:29-30

Suggested Reading

Romans 8:1-17
Luke 13:1-8
Acts 17:22-31
Revelation 2:1-7

"You will again have compassion on us. You will tread our sins underfoot and hurl all our iniquities into the depths of the sea."
Micah 7:19

Jill Chapman

Forgiveness

"And forgive us our debts as we forgive our debtors" Matthew 6:12

When Jesus taught the disciples to pray, he included forgiveness. The first part of the forgiveness prayer asks others to forgive us of our debts. Debts include monetary obligations, sins, and offenses. We teach children to apologize when they've done something wrong. As adults, we often forget to ask for forgiveness when we've done something wrong. When conflict arises, it can be easier to let it go or just avoid it altogether.

We can always go to the Lord for forgiveness. The prayer of forgiveness releases us from the debt of our offense. In many ways, it frees our soul from the burden of the mistake, so we are able to go to the person for reconciliation. Sometimes, the opportunity for an apology passes. Our minds can be free of the debt even when the other person doesn't acknowledge it.

Owing money often brings shame and regret. Sometimes, I avoid people after I've borrowed money from them and haven't paid it back. We can pray forgiveness for our debtors. This prayer of forgiveness releases any animosity we may feel toward the circumstances surrounding the debt. Whether the debt consists of money or mistakes, we don't have to carry the weight of shame and regret. We can pray for forgiveness.

KH

We often need to forgive the wrongs others have caused us. For me, this takes divine intervention. It can be difficult to move on after an argument, especially disagreements with close friends. The memories and hurt can last a lifetime if we don't surrender them in prayer. Prayers of forgiveness free us from the baggage we carry in our mistakes, conflicts, and disagreements.

> *"For if you forgive other people when they sin against you, your heavenly Father will also forgive you. But if you do not forgive others their sins, then your Father will not forgive your sins." (Matthew 6:14-15)*

Reflections

Is there someone that comes to mind that you need to forgive?

Do you need forgiveness from someone else?

Healing Prayers

"Shall I come and heal Him?" Matthew 8:7

The aloe plant is sometimes called the healing plant. People cut open the plant for the material beneath the thick skin of this succulent species. The inner parts of the aloe plant provide a key ingredient in products for skin, hair, and digestive care. You don't have to run to the pharmacy for these ingredients. If you own an aloe plant, you cut off a piece of it each time you need it. The plant heals itself by sealing itself and regrowing the cut areas.

Prayers of healing work like the aloe plant. Peter tells us that Jesus heals from His wounds (1 Peter 2:24). You can pray healing over any broken or diseased situation.

Like the aloe plant, Jesus can heal all that ails us. God desires to heal all our diseases (Psalms 103:3). We can pray for others to be healed (James 5:14).

Prayers of healing can go beyond the surface symptoms to the cause of pain. The fall of Adam and Eve brought sin into the world with all its brokenness, pain, and heartache. Jesus forgives our sins and brings emotional and spiritual healing (James 5:16; Psalms 147:3).

"Praise the Lord, my soul, and forget not all his benefits - who forgives all your sins and heals all your diseases" (Psalms 103:2-3)

Suggested Reading

James 5:13-16
Psalm 147

Cease Striving

"Cease striving and know that I am God. I will be exalted over the nations. I will be exalted over the earth" (Psalm 46:10 NASB 1995).

I took piano lessons throughout my childhood. My piano teacher made me keep track of my practice time in a little notebook. He wrote the assignment, and I tracked the time. I earned several little trophies by spending hours at the piano. One week, I ramped up my efforts for a particular song. The notes looked complicated and fast-paced. I wanted to impress my teacher with the beautiful piece. I worked tirelessly.

When I got to the lesson, I played my piece with confidence. I'd even memorized portions of it to avoid a break when I turned the page. However, I learned it wrong. Several spots were wrong. In the end, it took me longer to undo my bad habits from the extensive efforts than if I had just taken the time to get it right the first time.

> " It's not practice makes perfect. Practice makes practiced. Perfect practice makes perfect." My teacher knew my mistake without me having to explain. "

Perhaps we all do it. We push through when we should step aside and take a break. I thought more time would fix my tempo issues, but it took the whole piece off course. This is why the psalmist reminds us to "cease striving." In striving, we struggle to make things go our way.

KH

We devote serious efforts toward success when we just don't have to. "Know that I am God." We can rely on God to be faithful with the things we can't control.

As a writer, I take extra time to edit and add more hours to get the introduction just so. I send a few more emails to get the word out. I strive to control the market and the message of my work. In my personal life, I use careful planning with my family. I strive for perfection in housekeeping, party-making, and parenting. I add extra activities. More practice. The psalmist promises I can "cease striving," because God will make himself known. I don't have to do all of those things. I can trust God to do it for me.

Prayer

Today, I acknowledge that I don't have it all together. I'm relieved to know that I don't have to hold things together. You hold me together, Lord, and You are faithful to keep my family, my job, and household together.

I give up trying to do it all. Today, I surrender. I surrender my plans, my hopes, my finances. I surrender my husband and my children. I give you the arguments and the frustrations. I hand over the left-over dinner plates, the messy bedrooms, and the unpaid bills.

I'm tired of trying to please my inlaws. I'm worn out from cleaning my house and decorating to please the neighbors. I wear myself out in my striving. Today's the day I let it go.

Thank you for taking care of it all.

Jill Chapman

"This is the day the Lord has made. Let us REJOICE in it and be glad."

Psalm 118:24

Roots

Well, let me tell you a story about the way we grow
We're a lot like a little seed, don't you know.
If it's gonna be healthy and able to stand
It has got to have roots that's a part of the plan.

Well, we all start out as a little seed
Whether man or woman or flower or weed,
If the roots get damaged or broken apart
You just have to go back to the start.

'Cause the roots go down and the plant goes up
Just like the little seed in a cup.
And nobody really knows how or why,
But you can't change nature even if you try.

Now the secret in growing those healthy roots
Is the same as an apple or other fruits.
Put the seed where it's safe down inside the dirt
To protect and nurture and keep from hurt.

'Cause the roots go down and the plant goes up
Just like the little seed in a cup.
And nobody really knows how or why
We're all gonna live and we're all gonna die.

JMC

Now there's one big difference with the plant and me
Plants are earthly nature like the bird and bee.
When you ask Jesus Christ to come into your heart
The nature of God takes you back to the start.

'Cause the roots go down and the plant goes up
Just like the little seed in a cup
And nobody really knows how or why

BUT YOU CAN CHANGE NATURES IF YOU WANT TO TRY.

YOU **CAN** CHANGE NATURES IF YOU WANT TO TRY.

Psalms

"Sing praises to God, sing praises;
Sing praises to our King, sing praises." (Psalms 47:6).

I love music and singing. The quality of my voice does not influence my efforts to sing. I sing songs I know and love. I'll even attempt to sing the songs playing overhead at the grocery store, whether I know the lyrics or not.

God created music and songs. So, it doesn't surprise me that He put together a book of songs, Psalms. The book of Psalms includes songs of praise, thanksgiving, hardship, and trouble.

At times, I desire to pray, but find it difficult to think of the words. Psalms provide ideas for prayers. David poured out his heart to God through songs. I often read the Psalms as prayers.

Praying the Psalms allows me to express my feelings using God's Word. Sometimes, I adapt the language to modern situations.

Reflections

Do you have a favorite Psalm?

What songs do you sing when you praise God in your house?

KH

Praying Through Psalms

"The Lord is my strength and my shield;
my heart trusts in him, and he helps me,
My heart leaps for joy,
and with my song I praise him."
Psalms 28:7

Happiness

A prayer from Psalms 1

"Blessed is the one who does not walk in step with the wicked or stand in the way that sinners take or sit in the company of mockers" (Psalms 1:1)

Happiness comes from following Jesus. Lord, I know that to be true. I hate feeling like I'm in trouble. Sin carries a weight that I don't want to bear.

I will delight myself in the law of the Lord. I will spend my time reading my Bible and speaking Your praise. I will meditate on Your Word and not think about things that weigh me down.

You have promised to bless those who delight in You. Like a tree planted by the water (Psalm 1:3), You will bring me everything I need to thrive. You've said that I will prosper when I delight in You.

I know that it's not that way with the wicked. They never know what's going to happen next. They worry about money and jobs. They're devastated over relationship issues.

Watch over me, Lord. Keep me on the right path.

Suggested Reading

>Psalms 32
>Philippians 4:4-7
>Romans 12:9-21

KH

Peace

A prayer from Psalms 23

"Even though I walk through the darkest valley, I will fear no evil, for you are with me; your rod and your staff, they comfort me" (Psalms 23:4).

You are here with me, Lord Jesus, and you are much bigger than anything this living alone can throw at me. You assure me Your grace is sufficient, and so, Lord, I ask you for that grace, Your free and undeserved help. I seek Your peace, and I long to find rest in Your pasture as I walk along the caregiving path.

I call upon Your name, Jesus, to replace my anger with joy; my resentment with compassion, my fears with peace. Enter my days, Lord. Bring calm - the deep, absolute, and abiding peace which You alone can give.

Lord Jesus, I look to You and ask for Your guidance to help me move beyond my worries and concerns into the person You want me to be, someone who is filled with Your peace, Your understanding, and Your compassion.

Reflections

What do you worry about?

What thoughts play through your mind on repeat?

Consider making a list of requests (thoughts that keep coming) and give them to the Lord in prayer. Keep track of how He answers you.

JM

Strength From the Lord

A prayer from Psalms 29

"May the Lord give might to His people; may the Lord bless His people with peace" (Psalm 29:11, New American Bible Revised.)

Give to the Lord. Yes, today, I give to the Lord glory and might. He has done great things for me. The Lord provided dinner last night and coffee this morning. The Lord made a way for me. He brought me through hard times and wearisome trouble.

The voice of the Lord is over the waters. The God of glory thunders in power. He controls the wind, the waves, the storms, and the seasons. The Lord plants the fields and waters them. He sculpted the mountains and decorated them with trees.

Remember me, Lord, as I flee to you for protection.

"I have told you this that you might have peace in Me. In the world, you will have trouble, but take courage, I have conquered the world"
(John 16:33, NABR)

Suggested Reading

Joshua 2: 1-24
John 16:1-33
Acts 27: 13-26

JM

When I Feel Afraid

A prayer from Psalms 34

"I sought the Lord, and He answered me. He delivered me from all my fears" (Psalms 34:4)

I will praise the Lord and lift up His name at all times. When anxieties threaten to crush me, His praise will be on my lips. When depression pulls me down to the depths, I will rejoice in God, my Savior.

I will seek the Lord when I am afraid. I will call on His name when worry captures my mind. Jesus, my Rock, my Deliverer will rescue me again. He hears my cries for help and answers with deliverance.

He delivers me from all my fears.

I will not be afraid of people or things they could do to me. I refuse to be afraid of events that could happen. I will not entertain thoughts of horrible things happening to people I love.

No.

KH

I will only fear God. I will respect the Lord. He created the heavens and the earth. He holds eternity in the palms of His hands.

"The angel of the Lord encamps around those who fear Him, and He delivers them." (Psalms 34:7)

Suggested Reading

Psalms 56
Matthew 10:26-34
Mark 5:35-43

Life Seems Meaningless

A prayer from Psalms 39

"And now, Lord, for what do I wait? My hope is in You" (Psalm 39:7).

I need to put a muzzle on my mouth. I say the worst things, especially around certain people. When I keep my mouth shut, the words pile up in my mind. It's like I'm building a bonfire.

Lord, how much longer do I have to do this? This life is meaningless. How much longer do I have to endure it?

The Lord helps me look back over my life. It's short. The days get shorter. Surely, we're all running out of time. Everyone runs around trying to get as much money and things before they die, but it mounts up and means nothing.

What am I waiting for?

My hope is in the Lord. Deliver me, Lord, from the meaningless gathering of things. Deliver me from empty words and broken promises. Deliver me from comparison and insecurity.

Reflections

What needs to happen before you can have peace?

What are you waiting for?

Where is your hope? (A new job? A spouse? Recovery from illness?)

It's never too late to hope in Jesus.

KH

Longing for the Lord

A prayer from Psalms 42

> *"Deep calls to deep at the sound of Your waterfalls. All Your breakers and waves have rolled over me" (Psalms 42:7).*

As the deer searches and longs for water, I long to see God. My soul searches and longs for God, the living God.

Where are you?

I've been crying myself to sleep. I can still taste the tears. People mock me for trusting You. "Where's your God now?" They say.

I remember going to church with friends. We got together for Bible studies. It was so much fun.

Why do I get myself all worked up? God hasn't changed. I will hope in God. I will remember the things You've done for me. All the times You've come through for me.

From deep within me, I feel You calling me. Like the sound of a waterfall from a far distance, Your Spirit answers my prayers. I will hope in God. He will come through for me.

Suggested Reading

> Isaiah 55:1-13
> Matthew 5:6
> John 6:35-40

KH

God As My Refuge And Strength

A prayer from Psalms 46

> *"Therefore, we will not fear, though the earth give way and the mountains fall into the heart of the sea" (Psalms 46:2).*

God is a refuge, a place for me to hide in times of trouble. He's always ready to help me. Even if the earth falls apart, I won't be afraid. During horrible storms with winds that pull up trees, I will trust in God.

There is a river that brings life to the city of God. God is in the midst of it. He lives there. When He speaks, nature obeys the sound of His voice.

God is in control of it all. He makes wars stop. God brings peace to arguments and order into chaos. I will stop trying to control things. God can do it on His own. He will be exalted and praised.

Reflections

Where do you go to feel safe?

Who do you talk to during times of stress and hardship?

What things do you need to give to God?

KH

"Consider how the wild flowers grow. They do not labor or spin. Yet I tell you, not even Solomon in all his splendor was dressed like one of these."
Luke 12:27

Jill Chapman

My Enemies Pursue Me

A prayer from Psalms 56

> *"When I am afraid, I put my trust in you. In God, whose word I praise - in God I trust and am not afraid." (Psalms 56:3-4).*

Be merciful to me, Lord. My enemies chase me. Everywhere I go, they confront me. Some people really have it out for me. They spread rumors about me, and their gossip spreads all over town. I can't get away from it. They even convince others to hate me.

I can't trust anyone, but I trust You, Lord. You've shown Yourself to be faithful. You've never let me down.

They twist my words. When I make a statement or start a conversation, my enemies turn it into something horrible. It's like they're searching for mistakes.

I trust You, Lord. You won't let them get away with it. You love me and understand what I'm really trying to say. I can trust You to make things right.

You deliver me from empty threats and hateful comments. You rescue me from gossip and the sting of rejection. You, O Lord, accept me and love me.

Suggested Reading

Philippians 4
2 Timothy 1:6-11
1 John 4:7-18

KH

When Evil Wins

A Prayer from Psalm 73

"When You arise, Lord, You will despise them as fantasies" (Psalms 73:20).

It drives me crazy that the wicked people prosper. How can You let that happen? They don't have to worry about anything. I see them on social media. Their beautiful families and luxurious vacations. They don't have my problems.

Their children do well in school and get awards for sports. They've been married for a long time and enjoy spending their anniversary on beach vacations in Hawaii. Why don't they have my bills to pay? Why don't they need to go to counseling, or wish they could afford to do it? I don't see them wasting away in unemployment.

These people appear blessed, but I know the hate they preach. They speak evil of others. Always confrontational, they don't offer encouragement. They boast of their riches and mock the poor. They preach about righteousness and gossip when others aren't looking.

But I know their final destiny.

Your justice never fails, Lord. Surely, You're setting them up for ruin. Suddenly, they'll be destroyed and swept away by terrors.

KH

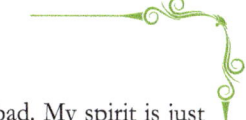

I was just like them. My words are just as bad. My spirit is just as bitter. I was senseless and ignorant.

Yet, I am always with You. You hold my right hand and guide me with Your Spirit. Nothing can compare with You. Earth has nothing for me.

> "My flesh and my heart may fail, but God is the strength of my heart and my portion forever" (Psalm 73:26).

Reflections

Where do you need God's strength today?

What places in life look like failures?

Where have you seen God's justice and provision?

When I Will Not Be Comforted

A Prayer from Psalm 77

"I will remember the deeds of the Lord. Yes, I will remember your miracles of long ago. I will consider all your works and meditate on all your mighty deeds (Psalms 77:11-12.)

On nights when I can't sleep, I call out to the Lord. I plead with Him for comfort. In my distress, the Lord reaches out His hands. I know He hears me and is with me.

But I'm still hurting.

I still can't sleep. I can't stop thinking about the painful things. I meditate on the Lord and His goodness.

But it still hurts.

I try to remember the things God has done. I start to write my praise, trying to be grateful to the Lord. I know He hears me.

But the pain won't go away.

How long will this last? Why am I so troubled? Why can't I get it together? It's time to speak His Word over it. That's it. I will declare the things of God from His Word.

KH

Your ways, God, are holy. There is no other god as great as my God.

You perform miracles. You displayed Your power among the peoples of the world. With Your mighty arm, You redeemed your people, Israel.

The waters saw you, God, and moved. The very depths obeyed Your voice.

Your path led through the sea. Your way through the mighty waters without footprints.

You led your people like a flock of sheep by the hand of Moses.

You can bring me out of this, too. I refuse to let emotions rule my life. I choose to trust in God. I will walk in His ways, even though my heart feels pain.

Suggested Reading

> Ephesians 4:17-32
> James 1:19-27

Patience

GROWS

"We must pay the most careful attention, therefore, to what we have heard, so that we do not drift away. For since the message spoken through angels was binding, and every violation and disobedience received its just punishment, how shall we escape if we ignore so great a salvation?"

Hebrews 2:1-3

Rescue

A Prayer from Psalm 91

> "Whoever dwells in the shelter of the Most High will rest in the shadow of the Almighty" (Psalms 91:1.)

Lord, You are my refuge and safe room, my God, in whom I trust.

You will save me from the traps of my enemies and from deadly diseases. You will stretch Your arms over me to hide me and protect me. Your faithfulness is a shield for me.

I will not be afraid of terrifying things. I will not worry about people breaking into my house to harm my family. I will not think about the safety of my family members as they travel or go about their days. I won't even worry about my teenager's driving. Cancer, heart disease, diabetes - none of them will cause me to fret.

A thousand may fall at my side, ten thousand at my right hand, but it won't come near me. I will watch the punishment of the wicked.

The Lord is my refuge. The Most High is my dwelling place.

No harm can overtake me. No disaster will take me out.

KH

You command your angels concerning me to guard me day and night. You say to me, *"Because I love you, I will rescue you. I will protect you because you acknowledge My name."*

O Lord, I know that when I call on You, You will answer me. You are with me when I am in trouble. You will deliver me and honor me. You will satisfy me with a long life to show me salvation.

Reflections

Is there any thing you are dealing with that you haven't brought to Jesus?

Where do you need God to intervene in your life?

Remembering the Benefits of the Lord

A Prayer from Psalm 103

"Praise the Lord, my soul, and forget not all his benefits". (Psalms 103:2.)

Praise the Lord. I will praise You from deep within me. I won't forget why I decided to follow Jesus.

You forgive all my sins and heal all my diseases.

You redeemed my life from the pit. You pulled me out of the worst situations. Even when I struggled with sin, You were there to bring me out. Not only did You pull me out, You crowned me with love and compassion.

You satisfy my desires. You give me the best things in life. I feel like a little kid at Christmas. You bring me such joy and happiness.

You work justice for the oppressed. I know that You will make things right. I don't have to worry about evil people getting away with it.

You are the same God that spoke to Moses on the mountain. The Lord is compassionate and gracious, slow to anger, and abounding in love. You treat me with kindness and never put me to shame. You don't accuse me of things. Instead, You offer forgiveness and freedom from guilt.

KH

For as high as the heavens are above the earth, so great is Your love for me. As far as the east is from the west, You have taken my sin - all of the things that are shameful about me - and removed them from me.

You treat me like a good father treats his children. You are patient with me, explaining things until I understand. You don't get upset with me when I don't understand what to do next. Instead, You wait with me, teaching me and helping me get it.

From everlasting to everlasting is Your love for me. You have always loved me, even before I knew You. There's nothing I can do to end Your love and affections for me.

Your throne is established in the heavens. Your kingdom rules over everything.

Praise the Lord, my soul.

Suggested Reading

> Isaiah 53:1-12
> Psalms 147:1-20
> James 5:13-20

You Know Me

A Prayer from Psalm 139

"You have searched me, Lord, and You know me" (Psalms 139:1.)

Lord, You know everything there is to know about me. You know my habits and plans. You can read my mind, because You know what I'm thinking.

When I get up in the morning, You know the first thing on my mind. You can predict where my thoughts will go next. You even know when I take naps. Before I say a word, You know what it's going to be. Sometimes, I don't even know that.

You are all around me. It's like when my grandma tucked me in with her thick, heavy quilts. I can't get away from Your Presence and protection. Your hand is on my life. Sometimes, it's too much for me. I can't understand it.

Where can I go to get away from you? Where can I hide? When I go dancing in the clubs, You're there. When I'm the only one who shows up for Bible study, You're there. Even if I boarded a spaceship to the moon, Your Presence would be there too. You'd guide the rockets to safety.

The darkness isn't dark to You. Night shines like day in Your eyes. When I'm trapped in uncertainty and scared, You are with me. It won't scare You. I can't keep secrets from You, Lord. I can't hide the words that have hurt me or the things I didn't mean to do. You know them, and You stay with me anyway.

KH

You created me - all the parts of me. You knew me before I was born. You planned out all my days before my mother knew about me. Your thoughts about me are kind and precious. I am always on Your mind. You don't forget about me.

Study me, Lord. Stay with me. Keep thinking about me. I need You. I need Your protection, safety, and comfort. So, study me. Tell me what I need to change and improve. Guide me in Your righteous way of living.

Reflections

How do you receive criticism?

What habits and thought patterns do you need to change?

Prayers from the Sermon on the Mount

"When Jesus saw the crowds, He went up on the mountain; and after He sat down, His disciples came to Him. He opened His mouth and began to teach them" (Matthew 5:1-2.)

Blessed Are The Poor In Spirit

A prayer from Matthew 5:3

> *"Blessed are the poor in spirit for theirs is the kingdom of heaven"*
> *(Matthew 5:3.)*

Thank you, Lord, for accepting me as I am. Thank you for loving me even when I am unable to love others around me. I confess today that I am hurting. Someone close to me (Insert the name here) broke my heart. I can't believe he said those things to me. The rejection makes me want to cut them out of my life forever.

I know that Jesus was also rejected by people close to Him (John 1:12.) You know how I feel, and I'm thankful that You sit with me in this pain.

Help me to forgive them.

Today, I choose to forgive (*Insert the name here*). I choose to release the pain that I hold because of what they did. Take my pain. Take my shame and regret. Jesus forgive them too. I ask you, Lord, to heal our relationship. Bring something good out of this situation.

Suggested Reading
Proverbs 15:31-33
Philippians 2:1-18
Colossians 3:12-17

KH

I Repent of My Efforts to Control My Life
A prayer from Acts 3:12-20

"Repent, then, and turn to God, so that your sins may be wiped out, that times of refreshing may come from the Lord" (Acts 3:19.)

Lord, I acknowledge the gift of salvation offered to me through the death and resurrection of Your Son, Jesus Christ. Forgive me of my sins. Today, I confess my unbelief. I haven't trusted You to care for me. I've spent too much time worrying about my job, my finances, and my loved ones. Forgive my lack of faith.

Today, I want to turn away from worry, fear, and anxiety. I'm making the decision not to trust in my ability to work things out. I'm walking away from the illusion of control that I hold dear. I recognize that I am powerless. I am nothing without Jesus (2 Corinthians 1:9.)

Today, I repent of my wicked ways, and I turn to God. I will put my trust in the One who Created me, the Sovereign God who is faithful to carry me. I trust the Lord, who will never fail me.

Reflections

Do you have people in your life that are controlling?

In what ways are you trying to control your own life?

KH

Forgive Me of My Debt

A prayer from Matthew 6:12

"And forgive us our debts as we forgive our debtors" (Matthew 6:12.)

Thank you, Lord, for walking with me in painful situations. I confess to you that I made another mistake. I'm in over my head this time. I borrowed money for a project at home, but I can't pay it back.

Forgive me for my poor planning. Help me to forgive myself for getting into this hole. Lord, I ask you to release me from the shame that I carry.

Transform the view I have of myself. When I see this debt, I see my failures and my inability to reconcile it. Rescue me from it, Lord. Free me from the weight of it.

Today, I forgive the people that I owe. Help me forgive the numerous phone calls and emails. I know they are only trying to collect the debt. Forgive me for lying to them on the phone. Forgive the careless words I say as I avoid talking to them. Remove the resentment that I have toward them. Give me forgiveness today, so that I can forgive them as well.

Suggested Reading

Isaiah 43: 18-28
Matthew 6:5-14
1 John 1:5-10

KH

"See, I have engraved you on the palms of my hands."

Isaiah 49:16

Dr. Kathy Hendley

Forgive Me for the Things I Said

A prayer from Luke 11:4

"If we confess our sins, he is faithful and just to forgive us our sins and to cleanse us from all unrighteiouness" (1 John 1:9.)

Lord, thank for accepting me along with all of my faults. I'm sorry for the way I treated *(fill in any name here)* the other day. I was wrong. I confess today that I am unable to treat others with kindness on my own. I need your help.

Forgive me for the awful words I said out loud, and forgive the other words left in my head. Forgive me for the things I did out of anger and frustration.

Take my hurt and my pain. Take my shame, please. I need Your peace once again. The regret fills my days and steals my sleep at night.

Forgive me, Lord. Help me avoid the temptation to do it again. Take my regrets and give me Your peace once again.

Reflections

What words do you wish you could take back?

Are there people in your life that encourage you to gossip?

What regrets do you need to hand over to Jesus today?

KH

Confessing My Sins and Seeking God's Face
A prayer from 2 Chronicles 7:14

"If My people who are called by My name will humble themselves, and pray and seek My face, and turn from their wicked ways, then I will hear from heaven, will forgive their sin and heal their land" (2 Chronicles 7:14.)

Lord, You control the world around me. I recognize that my sin carries consequences. Lord, You outlined the consequences of sin in the Law, and we know that sin brings death (Romans 6:23.) I confess that my life is a mess without You. I cannot manage my household, my finances, or my relationships without Your help. I have made a mess of things.

I confess that I've said horrible things to the people I love. My speech and actions have been abusive to the people I care about, but I can't stop hurting people. I cannot control my tongue without your help. I confess that I have made mistakes with my money. I spend too much on all the wrong things. I haven't given back to You or served You like You've asked of me.

Today, I want to change my ways. Lord, I want to see You. I'm turning to You for help. Help me with my words, my spending, and my habits. Reveal to me the changes I need to make. I want to serve You completely. I want to live my entire life to please You.

Suggested Reading
Ezra 10: 1-4
2 Chronicles 7:11-22
Mark 1: 4-8
James 5: 15-20

KH

Forgiving Someone Else

A prayer from Matthew 6:15

> *"But if you do not forgive men their trespasses, neither will your Father forgive your trespasses" (Matthew 6:15.)*

Thank you, Lord, for accepting me as I am. Thank you for loving me even when I am unable to love others around me. I confess today that I am hurting. Someone close to me, (Insert the name here), broke my heart. I can't believe he said those things to me. The rejection makes me want to cut them out of my life forever.

I know that Jesus was also rejected by people close to Him (John 1:12). You know how I feel, and I'm thankful that You sit with me in this pain.

Help me to forgive them.

Today, I choose to forgive (Insert the name here). I choose to release the pain that I hold because of what they did. Take my pain. Take my shame and regret. Jesus forgive them too. I ask you, Lord, to heal our relationship. Bring something good out of this situation.

Reflections

Sometimes, we need to name names. Who do you need to forgive today?

Saying that you forgive is easy. Changing your opinion of that person in your mind is difficult. Write a compliment or a prayer of blessing for someone that you forgive.

KH

Unity In My Marriage

A prayer from Philippians 2:7-9

Make my joy complete by being like-minded, having the same love, being one in spirit and of one mind" (Philippians 2:2).

Lord, I pray for my marriage. I pray that we would be united in spirit, intent on one purpose.

Let us do nothing from selfishness or arrogance, but give us humility. That we could regard one another as more important than ourselves. O Lord, help us not only look out for own interests, but also the interests of our spouse. Enable us to throw aside our personal comforts and desires for the sake of unity.

Lord, help me to consider my spouse's thoughts, cares, and concerns when we are together. Let me slow down. Let me listen to what he has to say.

Help us both to have the same attitude as Jesus Christ when He emptied Himself; became a man; and was obedient unto death. Let our obedience to Christ help us yield to one another and bring peace to our household.

Suggested Reading

>Ephesians 4:17-32
>Philippians 2:1-18
>Colossians 3: 1-17

KH

Unity Through Humility

A prayer from Ephesians 4:1-16

"Be completely humble and gentle; be patient, bearing with one another in love. Make every effort to keep the unity of the Spirit through the bond of peace." (Ephesians 4:2-3).

Lord Jesus, I confess that I'm not at peace. These people that I call family are driving me nuts. We can't seem to get along. We argue and fuss with each other. The little things cause heaps of frustration.

I love my family. I am thankful to have them in my life. Today, however, I feel ungrateful, irritated, frustrated, and full of shame and guilt.

I'm sorry for being selfish and wanting things done my way. I didn't wait to hear anyone else's ideas, plans, or dreams. I didn't ask about their thoughts or feelings. Honestly, I never considered their feelings in my actions or words to them. I want to look to You when I plan my schedule and set my expectations.

Forgive me. Forgive my anxious thoughts. Forgive me for filling up my and not making time for my family. Forgive my mean words, the curses and complaints that flowed from me in anger.

KH

Help me, Lord. Give me grace, so I can grow up. Fill me with the Holy Spirit and bring me a patient, quiet heart. Send me words of gratitude to share with my family.

Reflections

Confession involves recognizing where you stand in relation to God's commands. Where do you stand in relationship to your spouse?

Where do you need God to intervene in your marriage?

Jesus often referred to marriage in discussions about the kingdom of God. We are His bride. Where do you stand in relationship to Jesus?

KH

Encouragement
A Prayer from 1 Thessalonians 5

Rejoice always; pray continually; give thanks in all circumstances, for this is God's will for you in Christ Jesus" (1 Thessalonians 5:16).

Lord, You know that we all need to hear encouragement. We need our strengths to be named and appreciated. Help me to be a friend who acknowledges the good qualities in others.

On the other hand, I don't want to be the friend who is like a tightly wrapped umbrella. You think you can count on them until the rain begins to fall and you find yourself soaked to the skin. Help me to be a friend who is not afraid to warn others about sin or failures.

Lord, I want to love others actively. So actively, that I speak both words of challenge and words of hope. Let me be the one who rejoices always, prays continuously, and give thanks in all circumstances.

"The tongue that brings healing is a tree of life" (Proverbs 15:3).

Suggested Reading

I Thessalonians 5
Titus 2: 1-15
2 Timothy 4: 1-5

JM

The Light

A prayer from John 3:16-21

"For God so loved the world that he gave his one and only Son, that whoever believes in him shall not perish but have eternal life" (John 3:16).

Thank you, Lord, for sending light into this dark world. Lord, You remember when I was scared of the dark. Even now, I run into the dark all the time. Dark thoughts enter my mind and bring destruction. The fear causes me to freeze.

Thank you for sending the Light.

Thank you for sending Your Son, Jesus, to be Light in this darkness. You sent Him to bring Light and salvation for all of us. I thank you, Lord, because I know that when I call on the name of Jesus the darkness flees. You save me from dark thoughts and fear. You shed light on my problems and pains. You save me from myself in so many ways.

Thank you for the truth that comes from Jesus. Thank you for delivering me from darkness.

Reflections

What has Jesus done for you? Where has His Light brought you healing and help?

Where do you need light today?

JM

Prayers for Waiting on God

"Wait for the Lord; be strong and take heart
and wait for the Lord" (Pslams 27:14).

God is Good

A prayer from 1 Thessalonians 5:18

"Give thanks in all circumstances; for this is God's will for you in Christ Jesus" (1 Thessalonians 5:18).

The Lord is good. No matter what happens. I choose to give thanks. I will shout out loud that God is good.

"God is good!"

I will tell others of God's faithfulness. The Lord has delivered me from evil. He brought me into His kingdom of peace with forgiveness.

"God is good!"

I am thankful for His lovingkindness towards me. No matter what life throws at me, I know that I am safe in Christ.

"God is good!"

I choose to be thankful. I will turn my focus on Jesus Christ who cares for me. Thank you, Lord, for loving me and choosing me. Thank you for accepting me into Your kingdom. Thank you for giving me hope.

Suggested Reading
Psalms 118
Psalms 136
2 Corinthians 1: 1-11

KH

Healing My Fears

A prayer from Job 11:13-20

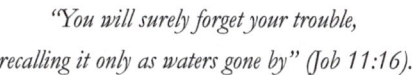

*"You will surely forget your trouble,
recalling it only as waters gone by"* (Job 11:16).

As I lay down to sleep, I read this over and over until I fall asleep:

I am secure and fed.

I'm confident because there is hope.

Yes, I look around me and take my rest in safety.

I lie down, and no one makes me afraid.

"You will be secure, because there is hope; You will look about you and take your rest in safety. You will lie down, with no one to make you afraid, and many will court your favor" (Job 11:18-19.)

Reflections

What troubles you today? You can ask God to take it from you.

What is your hope?

Write this verse in a place you will see it. Take a photo and set it as the wallpaper in your phone. Remind yourself throughout the day.

JM

Holy Armor

A prayer from Ephesians 6

"Put on the full armor of God so that you can take your stand against the devil's schemes" (Ephesians 6:11).

Father God, I thank You for Your patience in loving and leading me. Help me to follow Your example with others.

I need the Armor You provide to get me through each day.

Thank You for protecting my mind & thoughts with the helmet, and my heart & emotions with the **breastplate of righteousness.**

Thank You for the **belt of truth** which allows me to discern Truth and recognize the enemies lies.

Thank You for Your Word, my **sword** and my weapons of worship & prayer.

Thank You for the **shield of faith** and **gospel of peace** on my feet wherever I go.

Remind me that everyone I encounter has worth. Let Your Holy Spirit guide me. Let ALL I do reflect my love for You.

JMC

Examine me, test my ways (Psalm26:2) to remind me I'm in need of Your Amazing Grace. You are enough! For **today**, make me unoffendable & grateful.

Thank you for providing this gift of armor for me. I ask you to cover my entire family. (*Name specific people here*). Your helmet protects our minds. The breastplate guards our hearts and emotions. Jesus is our belt - the way, the truth, and the life - our help to discern enemies. Your shield hems me in behind and covers all of me. The shoes of peace carry the gospel and my testimony everywhere I go.

Thank you for the **sword**, my defense.

Reflections

Consider covering yourself with the amor listed above.

Find scriptures to use for defense against temptations from the enemy.

Courage to Trust

A prayer from Proverbs 3

"When you lie down, you will not be afraid.
When you lie down, your sleep will be sweet...for the Lord will be at your side
and will keep your foot from being snared." (Proverbs 3:24, 26).

Heavenly Father, be patient with me. It is my nature to want all the answers and to be able to give directions to solve the issues I see today, as well as, those that could happen tomorrow. I awaken with worry and go to bed with worry.

Help me to turn to you with all these thoughts that occupy so much of my mind and place them into your hands. Give me the courage, Lord, to let these things go and to trust you with them.

May I begin to see the purpose in what I encounter each day. Shield me from worry. Show me how to get comfortable with using all that you give me today wisely, knowing that you already have tomorrow.

Suggested Reading

Psalms 40: 1-17
Proverbs 3: 1-26
Romans 8: 18-30

JM

Holy Spirit

A prayer from John 20

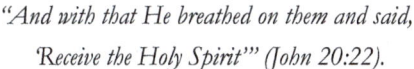

"And with that He breathed on them and said,
'Receive the Holy Spirit'" (John 20:22).

Breathe into me, Holy Spirit, that my thoughts may all be holy.

Move in me, Holy Spirit, that my work, too, may all be holy.

Attract my heart, Holy Spirit, that I may love only what is holy.

Strengthen me, Holy Spirit, that I may defend all that is holy.

Protect me, Holy Spirit, that I may always be holy.

"And the disciples were filled with joy
and with the Holy Spirit" (Acts 13: 52.)

Reflections

Where do you need help from the Holy Spirit today?

How has the Holy Spirit helped you in the past?

JM

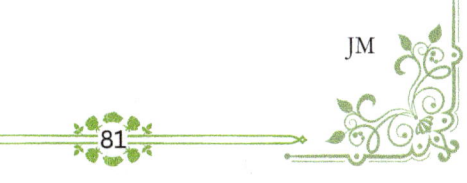

Wisdom

A prayer from James 1

"If any of you lacks wisdom, you should ask God, who gives generously to all without finding fault, and it will be given to you" (James 1:5).

You walk before me and you know every decision I will need to make. Yet, I feel lost and uncertain at times. There are situations and choices in my day. I am afraid to make the wrong decision and do not know who I trust to help me.

Jesus, I need you. I ask only for Your will to be done. Have mercy on me when I forget to stop and pray before I act. Let me lean on You. Let the Holy Spirit speak to me. I need wisdom that can come only from You.

As I awaken each morning, I will turn to You for I know that You will carry me through this journey. Help me to recognize and rejoice in the blessings you reveal to me along the way.

Reflections

What mistakes have you made lately? Ask God for wisdom in those areas.

What waa the first thing you asked God for this morning?

JM

Timing

A prayer from Ecclesiastes 3

> *"There is a time for everything and a season for every activity under the heavens" (Ecclesiastes 3:1).*

Sometimes one day just blurs into the next.

Time is precious. We know that, yet time can slip away.

I live in survival mode most of the time! I find myself wishing time away while dreading what tomorrow might bring. This sometimes can make it difficult to see the precious moments God gives me.

God, give me glimpses of the precious time I have left. I live only for today.

The reality is there are only three places you can live: the past, the present, or the future. The past is gone. God asks me to leave it behind.

> *"Remember not the events of the past, the things of long ago consider not"(Isaiah 43:18).*

JM

The future is also out of my reach. I cannot live there either.

*Do not worry about tomorrow,
tomorrow will take care of itself (Matthew 6:34).*

God goes before me to pave my path. It is filled with all that I need for Today.

Suggested Reading

Acts 1: 7-8
Galatians 6:7-10
1 Peter 5: 1-11

About the Authors

"We must pay the most careful attention, therefore, to what we have heard, so that we do not drift away. For since the message spoken through angels was binding, and every violation and disobedience received its just punishment, how shall we escape if we ignore so great a salvation?"

Hebrews 2:1-3

Kathy Hendley, PhD

Dr. Kathy Hendley is a teacher, author, and speaker. She enjoys playing keyboard at her church, reading a good mystery novel, and searching the globe for Bible studies. Kathy's mission is to encourage others to overcome obstacles, achieve their goals, and commit to their calling. Prayer has changed her life, and Kathy believes that prayer can change anything. You can connect with Kathy through her website at kathyhendley.com

Jean McMullin

Jean McMullin is a teacher, Bible study enthusiast, and ultimate prayer warrior. She collaborated on this book with her daughter, Dr. Kathy Hendley. She is a clear inspiration to her children and grandchildren.

Kristina R. Wise

Passionate speaker, educator and dynamic Bible teacher, Kristina has a mission to help women live their lives through God's Word. Kristina has written devotional publications for various women's ministries including books: *Strength in Him* and *Daily Devos with Kristina*. She currently co-hosting the podcast, "Bible Study Besties." Kristina also teaches her own online Bible Study. Follow Kristina on her journey at www.kristinareneexo.com and instagram @kristinareneexo

Jill Chapman

Jill resides in Southern Indiana with her husband of forty-six years. As a writer and speaker, she loves to tell stories about her life experiences, mixing humor into her positive messages of God's love to convey the sense of adventure she feels every day. Jill says her life is like a good plate of nachos: a tiny kick of spice and a whole lotta cheese.

Connect with Jill at her website authorjillchapman.com

Jeanie Connell

Jeanie is an author, Song Writer, and Speaker. She is currently publishing 52 Children's Devotions titled, *God Likes Kids*. Her memoir published by Selah Press came out on Amazon in 2022: *Promise You Won't Remember – Becoming Whole When Pieces are Missing*. Jeanie is certified with the American Association of Christian Counselors.

Her books and songs reflect her deep love of prayer. She and her husband Michael live in Cartersville, GA. Connect with Jeanie at www.jeanieconnell.com

Prayers and Praises

Prayers and Praises

Prayers and Praises

Prayers and Praises

www.ingramcontent.com/pod-product-compliance
Lightning Source LLC
Chambersburg PA
CBHW060848050426
42453CB00008B/888